The Big Book of Financial Literacy for Teenagers

Vandana Verma

AF519910

DIAMOND BOOKS

www.diamondbooks.in

Publisher	**:**	**Diamond Pocket Books (P) Ltd.** X-30, Okhla Industrial Area, Phase-II New Delhi-110020
Phone	:	011-40712200
E-mail	:	wecare@diamondbooks.in
Website	:	www.diamondbooks.in
Edition	:	2025
Printed By	:	Repro (India)

Preface

Money is not just about numbers—it's about making smart decisions that shape your future. In today's world, teenagers are exposed to money earlier than ever, whether through pocket money, part-time work, digital wallets, or social media. Yet, financial literacy is often ignored in classrooms and homes.

This book was written to change that. "Smart Teen Ki Smart Money Guide" is designed especially for Indian teenagers, aligning with the National Education Policy (NEP) 2020, NCF 2023, and CBSE skill development goals. It gives you real-world tools, relatable stories, and practical activities that will help you understand, manage, and grow your money wisely.

From budgeting and saving to investing and entrepreneurship, this guide is your first step toward financial confidence and independence.

- Vandana Verma

Foreword

In a world where teenagers can earn, spend, invest, and create online businesses from their phones, understanding money is not optional—it's essential. Yet, many teens graduate school without knowing how to create a budget, avoid debt traps, or invest for their dreams.

This book arrives as a much-needed revolution in youth education. It speaks to teenagers in their language while empowering them to plan for life's goals with confidence. I commend the authors for presenting finance in a way that's not intimidating but exciting.

This is not just a guidebook—it's a roadmap to becoming financially smart, socially responsible, and future-ready. Read it, reflect on it, and start applying it today.

Contents

Chapter 1

Why Financial Literacy Matters for Teens

Meet Ria. She's 15 and dreams of buying a new bicycle worth ₹6,000. Every month she saves ₹200 from her allowance. But with festival season around the corner, her savings keep shrinking. One day her friend suggests borrowing money, while her older cousin advises investing it instead. Ria is confused—should she borrow, save more, or try investing?

This is exactly where financial literacy comes in. It's not just about money—it's about knowing how to make smart decisions, avoid mistakes, and plan for your dreams. The sooner you learn about it, the better your life will be.

Explore: What is Financial Literacy?

Financial literacy means understanding how money works and how to manage it wisely.

It includes knowing how to:
- Budget your money
- Save for goals
- Spend smartly
- Use banking tools
- Understand credit and debt
- Start investing
- Plan for your future

In short, it's learning how to make money work for you, not the other way around.

Why Teens Need It Now

In the past, teenagers mostly dealt with cash and piggy banks. But today, you're surrounded by digital wallets, UPI apps, shopping websites, social media ads, and instant purchases. You probably get pocket money, gifts, or even earn from tutoring, creating content, or internships.

Without financial literacy, you might:
- Spend everything impulsively
- Fall for peer pressure purchases
- Ignore saving until it's too late
- Get into debt early (credit traps, BNPL schemes)
- Struggle with future goals like college, a vehicle, or your first job

Real-Life Examples of Teen Money Mistakes

- Tanya, 16, spent her Diwali gift money on a branded hoodie that was trendy for just a week. Now she regrets not saving for a laptop upgrade.
- Ankur, 17, used a "Buy Now Pay Later" offer for wireless earbuds, not realizing it added interest. He's now paying double the original price.

• Mehak, 15, saved ₹10,000 over a year and invested it in a risky crypto app without research. The app shut down, and she lost it all.

These are real stories that happen every day. But with the right skills, you can avoid them.

Common Money Myths Teens Believe

Myth	Truth
"I'm too young to care about money."	You're already earning and spending—this is the time to learn.
"I don't need to budget unless I have a salary."	Budgeting works for any amount—₹100 or ₹10,000.
"Saving is boring and slow."	Saving is what gives you the power to buy what matters most.
"Only rich people need to invest."	Anyone can start investing—many platforms start at ₹100.

Try It: Your Money Story

Take a notebook or your phone and answer:

1. When was the first time you received money on your own?
2. What did you do with it?
3. Was it a good decision? Would you do it differently today?
4. Do you track how much you spend weekly or monthly?
5. What's the last thing you regretted buying?

Reflection builds awareness. Once you know your habits, you can improve them.

How Financial Choices Shape Your Life

You may not realize it now, but the way you handle money today will impact:

- Your college choices and whether you can afford them
- Your ability to buy gadgets, bikes, or even start a business
- Your mental health (money stress is real)
- Your independence as an adult

Let's Learn from the Pros

Even celebrities and successful entrepreneurs started learning young.

- Warren Buffett, one of the world's richest investors, bought his first shares at age 11.
- Kiran Mazumdar-Shaw, India's biotech pioneer, talks about managing her earnings from her first job to build Biocon.
- Many teen creators and coders on YouTube earn ₹5,000–₹20,000 a month—some invest, others waste it.

The difference? Financial literacy.

Think & Reflect

Ask yourself honestly:

- What does "financial freedom" mean to me?
- Do I want to depend on my parents forever?
- What kind of life do I want at age 25? 35?
- How can smart money choices get me there?

Write your answers and revisit them every 3–6 months.

Let's Revise – Key Takeaways

- Financial literacy is about managing money wisely—earning, spending, saving, and investing.
- You are already dealing with money as a teenager, so this is the

perfect time to learn.

- Ignorance leads to mistakes like debt, impulse spending, or failed goals.
- Building good habits now creates a strong foundation for your future.

Check Yourself – Mini Quiz

1. What is financial literacy?
a) Learning how to become rich
b) Understanding and managing money smartly
c) Spending without thinking
d) Only investing in crypto
Correct answer: b

2. What happens if you spend impulsively without a plan?
a) You become famous
b) You save more
c) You risk running out of money and regret purchases
d) You get rich faster
Correct answer: c

3. True or False:
"I can wait until I'm an adult to care about finances."
Correct answer: False

Beyond the Book – Explore More

Apps:

- Walnut – Track spending
- Money Manager – Budget easily
- FamZoo – Family budgeting for teens

Videos:

- "Money Skills for Teens" – Khan Academy
- "How to Build Wealth in Your Teens" – CA Rachana Ranade

Books:
• "I Want More Pizza" – A fun guide for teens
• "The Teen Money Manual" – Smart tips and relatable stories

Websites:
• mymoney.gov
• younginvestor.gov

Teen Voices

Shivani, 15 (Delhi):
"I used to spend my money on food and random things. Now I save for a guitar. Every ₹100 saved feels like a step closer to my dream."

Aarush, 16 (Pune):
"I started using a budget app to see where my money goes. Turns out I was spending ₹800/month on snacks! I cut that in half and started saving."

Final Word

Financial literacy isn't a boring adult topic. It's your superpower.

It helps you:
• Make smarter daily decisions
• Say "yes" to the things that matter
• Avoid money stress
• Build a life of confidence and freedom
Start small. Learn weekly. Ask questions. Save with purpose. You don't need to be perfect—just aware, honest, and willing to improve. Because the smartest teen isn't the one with the fanciest phone—it's the one who knows how to use money to create a better life.

Chapter 2

Understanding Money

Earning, Spending, Saving

Aryan is 16. He gets ₹1,200 per month as pocket money. He sometimes earns extra by tutoring his neighbor's kid. But at the end of every month, he barely has anything left. When asked where it went, he shrugs and says, "I don't really know."

Sound familiar?

Many teens like Aryan are earning and spending, but very few are actually tracking, planning, or saving. This chapter is your first deep dive into how money flows—and how to take charge of it.

Explore: What Is Money and Where Does It Come From?

Money is more than just notes and coins—it's a tool that allows us to buy things, pay for services, and exchange value.

How do teens earn money?

Even if you're not employed, you may still be earning in several ways:
• Allowance from parents
• Gifts (festivals, birthdays)
• Part-time jobs (tutoring, babysitting, freelancing)
• Pocket money for chores
• Online content creation (YouTube, art, e-books)
• Prize money or scholarships
Earning teaches responsibility. When you work for your money, you're more likely to respect it.

What Do Teens Spend Money On?

Your expenses might include:
• Snacks and food delivery
• Online shopping
• Mobile data packs or subscriptions (Spotify, Netflix, etc.)
• Clothes, accessories
• Gifts for friends or family
• Games, digital content

These aren't "bad" expenses—but unplanned spending can create problems like:
• Running out of money early
• Not having enough for something important later
• Borrowing unnecessarily

The Cycle: Earn → Spend → Save... or Save First?

Most people follow this pattern:
Earn → Spend → Save (if anything is left)

But smart teens flip it to:
Earn → Save first → Spend what's left

This idea is called "Pay Yourself First"—we'll revisit it in budgeting.

Understanding Wants vs. Needs

This is a superpower skill.

Needs (Must-Haves)	**Wants (Nice-To-Haves)**
Bus pass	Uber ride
School uniform	Branded T-shirt
Notebooks, pens	Fancy stationery
Healthy lunch	Junk food

Every time you spend, ask: "Do I need this or just want it?"
Smart spending doesn't mean no fun—it means spending with awareness.

What Is Saving?

Saving is the act of setting money aside for the future instead of spending it right away.

Why should teens save?
- To buy something big (a phone, a laptop, a cycle)
- For college or coaching classes
- For emergencies
- For gifts or travel
- To feel independent and responsible

Even ₹50–₹100 saved every week adds up over time!

How to Start Saving?

1. Set a small goal (e.g., "Save ₹1,000 in 2 months")
2. Decide how much to save weekly or monthly
3. Track your progress (use apps or a notebook)

4. Put savings in a separate place (piggy bank, second wallet, savings account)
5. Avoid dipping into it unless necessary

The Magic of Compound Interest

Let's say you save ₹500 every month.

In one year:
₹500 × 12 = ₹6,000
Now, if that amount is put in a savings or investment account earning interest, the money grows without you doing anything.
This is called compound interest—earning interest on your interest.

Example:
₹10,000 invested at 7% annually =
- ₹700 interest in Year 1
- ₹749 interest in Year 2 (on ₹10,700)
- ₹801 in Year 3 (on ₹11,449)

The earlier you start saving, the more time your money has to grow.

Try It: Money Tracker Challenge

For the next 7 days, track every rupee you:
- Earn
- Spend
- Save

Use any method:
- A notebook
- A Google Sheet
- A mobile app (like Walnut or Money Manager)

At the end of 7 days, answer:
- How much did I spend?

• What category ate up most of my money?
• How much did I save?
• What could I cut down next week?

Think & Reflect

• If I had saved every ₹20 I spent on junk food last month, how much would I have?
• What's one "want" I can skip this week to reach my goal?
• What would it feel like to buy something I love using my own saved money?

Let's Revise – Key Takeaways

• Teens earn money from multiple sources—not just jobs
• Spending isn't bad, but unplanned spending hurts your goals
• **Always ask:** Is this a need or a want?
• Saving gives you freedom, security, and satisfaction
• Start early and let compound interest grow your money

Check Yourself – Mini Quiz

1. What's the smarter order to manage money?
a) Earn → Spend → Save
b) Earn → Save → Spend
c) Earn → Borrow → Spend
d) Earn → Spend → Lend
Correct answer: b

2. Which of these is a need, not a want?
a) Limited-edition sneakers
b) School books
c) Birthday party decor
d) Headphones for gaming
Correct answer: b

3. True or False:
Saving only ₹100 a month doesn't make a difference.
Correct answer: False (Small amounts build big habits!)

Beyond the Book – Explore More

Apps to Try:

- Walnut – Expense tracking
- Money Lover – Budgeting with visuals
- Splitwise – To manage shared spending with friends

Watch:

- "How Teens Can Build Saving Habits" – Khan Academy
- "Why Compound Interest Is Magic" – YouTube Shorts

Read:

- "The Barefoot Investor (Teen Edition)"
- "Money Matters: A Teen Guide"

Try:
Start a monthly savings challenge with a friend—whoever saves more wins a reward!

Real Teen Voices

Riya, 14 (Ahmedabad):
"I started saving ₹100 a week for a smartwatch. Now, I'm halfway there and proud I didn't ask my parents for it."

Yuvraj, 17 (Guwahati):
"My cousin told me about compound interest. I opened a small FD with my birthday money. It feels cool watching it grow."

Final Word

Understanding how you earn, spend, and save is the foundation of financial success.

You don't need a job or a salary to start managing money. You just need to be aware, track your actions, and set goals.

Every rupee saved today brings you one step closer to your dream tomorrow.

Now that you know how money works—are you ready to build your first budget?

Chapter 3

Making a Budget

Your First Money Plan

Say hello to Mehak. She earns ₹800 a month from tutoring and gets ₹500 as pocket money. Yet, by the 20th of every month, her wallet is empty. When asked where her money went, she says, "I think I spent a little here and there… I'm not sure." Sound familiar?

Most teens don't track their spending. But when you learn how to make a budget, it's like putting your money on a map—you know where it's coming from, where it's going, and how to get to your goals.

Explore: What Is a Budget and Why Do You Need One?

A budget is simply a plan for your money.

It helps you decide:

• How much you'll save

• What you'll spend on
• Where you need to cut back
It's not about restriction—it's about direction.
Imagine going on a road trip without a GPS. You might reach your destination eventually, but you'd probably waste time, money, and energy. A budget is your financial GPS.

Why Every Teen Needs a Budget

• You're already handling money (allowance, earnings, gifts)
• You face daily choices (Starbucks or savings?)
• You may have savings goals (new phone, laptop, trip)
• You'll soon face bigger financial decisions (college, transport, living expenses)

Budgeting teaches you how to balance needs and wants, avoid unnecessary borrowing, and feel in control of your financial life.

Key Budgeting Terms You Should Know

Term	**Meaning**
Income	Money you receive (allowance, part-time work, gifts)
Expenses	Money you spend (food, subscriptions, stationery, entertainment)
Fixed Costs	Regular costs that don't change much (school fees, bus pass)
Variable Costs	Expenses that change month to month (eating out, gifts, shopping)
Savings	Money you set aside before you spend anything else
Surplus	Leftover money after you meet all expenses
Deficit	When your expenses are more than your income (not ideal!)

Popular Budgeting Methods for Beginners

1. The 50-30-20 Rule

Break your after-tax income like this:
- 50% Needs (food, school, transport)
- 30% Wants (eating out, clothes, fun)
- 20% Savings

If you earn ₹1,500 a month:
- ₹750 = Needs
- ₹450 = Wants
- ₹300 = Savings

2. Pay Yourself First

As soon as you get money:
1. Save a fixed amount first (e.g., ₹200/month)
2. Then plan how to spend the rest

This method builds strong savings habits.

3. The Envelope Method

Old school, still powerful:
- Label envelopes (Food, Travel, Shopping, Savings)
- Allocate cash accordingly
- Spend only what's in each envelope

You can do this digitally too—with budgeting apps like Goodbudget or Walnut.

Try It: Build Your First Budget

Take a notebook or spreadsheet and do this:
Step 1: Write down your total income.
Example:

• Pocket money = ₹500
• Part-time tutoring = ₹1,000
Total = ₹1,500

Step 2: Estimate your monthly expenses.

Category	**Item**	**Amount**
Needs	Bus fare	₹400
	School lunch	₹300
Wants	Movies	₹200
	Snacks	₹250
Savings	New phone goal	₹350

Total Expenses = ₹1,500
If it doesn't add up? Adjust the wants first—not your savings!

Common Budgeting Mistakes (and How to Avoid Them)

Mistake	**Fix**
Forgetting small daily expenses	Track even ₹10 tea or chips—it adds up!
Not planning for emergencies	Add an "unexpected" category in your budget
Skipping savings completely	Always save something, even ₹100
Borrowing to overspend	Stick to your budget—don't spend money you don't have

Think & Reflect

• What's the one thing I always overspend on?
• Have I ever felt regret after spending without thinking?
• What would happen if I budgeted for the next 30 days?
• How much would I save in 3 months if I cut one junk food item a week?

Write your answers in a journal or phone note. Review it monthly.

Let's Revise – Key Takeaways

• A budget is a plan for your money—giving it purpose and direction
• Budgeting is not about limits—it's about choices and priorities
• Use tools like the 50-30-20 rule or envelope method to stay organized
• Always save first—it's your ticket to financial independence
• Budgeting builds discipline, self-control, and peace of mind

Check Yourself – Mini Quiz

1. What is the 50-30-20 rule?
a) Spend 50% on wants, 30% on savings, 20% on needs
b) Save 50%, spend 30%, donate 20%
c) 50% needs, 30% wants, 20% savings
d) No rule exists
Correct answer: c

2. Which budgeting method involves labeling money into categories?
a) Credit score method
b) SIP investing
c) Envelope method
d) Fixed deposit plan
Correct answer: c

3. True or False:
You should plan to save after spending what you need.
Correct answer: False (You should save first!)

Beyond the Book – Tools & Resources

Apps to Try:

- Goodbudget – Envelope-style budgeting
- Walnut – Indian app to track expenses
- Money Lover – Tracks budgets and savings goals

Templates to Download:

- Google Sheets Budget Template for Teens
- Printable Monthly Budget Tracker (make your own)

Watch:

- "How to Create a Budget for Beginners" – YouTube (Khan Academy)
- "Budgeting Tips for Students" – CA Rachana Ranade

Read:

- "Money Sense for Teens" by Kelley Keehn
- "Smart Budgeting" – Free eBook from Investopedia

Real Teen Voices

Ishaan, 15 (Hyderabad):
"I used to run out of money by the second week. Once I started budgeting, I realized I was spending too much on delivery food. Now I plan my snacks and save ₹300 every month!"

Sneha, 17 (Chennai):
"My budget helped me buy my own headphones in 4 months. I felt proud because I didn't need to ask anyone else for money."

Final Word

Budgeting isn't just for adults—it's a life skill every teenager needs. When you know where your money is going, you control your future. Whether your goal is a new phone, college savings, or just managing your money better, a budget is your best friend. Start now, keep it simple, and watch your confidence (and savings!) grow.

Chapter 4

Banking Basics

Your First Step to Financial Freedom

Zoya, age 16, receives ₹2,000 as a Rakhi gift from her brother. Her dad says, "Don't just keep it in your drawer—open a bank account!"

But Zoya has questions:
What kind of account?
Will the bank allow her to open one as a minor?
What is a passbook or a UPI?
Can someone steal her money online?

If you've ever felt unsure about how banks work, this chapter is your answer. Understanding banking basics is your first real step into the world of smart money management.

Explore: What Is a Bank and What Does It Do?

A bank is more than a place to deposit money—it's your partner in financial growth.

It helps you:

- Keep your money safe
- Earn interest on savings
- Access money anytime via ATM, app, or UPI
- Pay others quickly and securely
- Learn discipline and responsibility

Why Should Teens Use a Bank?

Even if you're still in school, a bank account helps you:

- Track your spending
- Set savings goals (e.g., new phone, coaching fee)
- Learn how digital payments work
- Build habits of financial planning early
- Feel independent and trusted

Types of Bank Accounts (And What They Mean)

Account Type	**Purpose & Features**
Savings Account	For saving money; earns interest; comes with ATM card & online banking
Current Account	Used by businesses; no interest; higher transaction limits
Fixed Deposit (FD)	One-time deposit for a fixed period; earns higher interest than savings account
Recurring Deposit (RD)	Monthly fixed deposit for a chosen time frame; promotes saving discipline
Minor Account	Special savings account for people under 18; requires a parent or guardian to open

For teens, a minor savings account is ideal—most banks offer this with great features and low or zero minimum balance.

What You Need to Open a Bank Account as a Teen

You typically need:

• Aadhaar card (yours and a parent's)
• PAN card (or Form 60 if unavailable)
• Passport-size photo
• Guardian's signature for minors

Banks like SBI, HDFC, Bank of Baroda, and ICICI all offer teen-friendly accounts.

Banking Tools You Should Know

Tool	What It Does
ATM/Debit Card	Withdraw cash, pay in shops, check balance
Passbook	Paper record of deposits, withdrawals, and interest
Netbanking	Access your bank account online
Mobile Banking App	Check balance, transfer money, pay bills
UPI (Unified Payments Interface)	Instantly send/receive money via phone apps

Popular UPI & Banking Apps for Teens

• PhonePe, Google Pay, Paytm – UPI payments and wallet features
• YONO (SBI) – Teen savings and investment tools
• HDFC Bank Kids App – Special dashboards for saving and spending
• FamPay – Prepaid cards and UPI access for teens without bank accounts

Always enable app lock and UPI PIN protection for safety.

Safety First – How to Use Banking Tools Wisely

1. NEVER share your ATM PIN, OTP, or UPI code.
2. Avoid public Wi-Fi when doing online banking.
3. Use strong passwords for mobile banking apps.
4. Don't click links in unknown messages or emails.
5. Review account statements monthly for unknown charges.

Try It: Banking Role Play

Activity: Open Your "Mock" Bank Account

On a sheet of paper or in a digital doc:
• Name of your bank
• Your starting deposit (e.g., ₹1,000 from pocket money)
• Create 3 fake transactions: Deposit, Spend, Save
• Track your balance after each
This helps you visualize how banking works in real life.

Think & Reflect

• What do I currently do with the money I receive?
• Am I using a bank to save and grow it?
• How can I start my digital banking journey with safety and discipline?

Let's Revise – Key Takeaways

• A bank account is your financial foundation
• Teens can open minor savings accounts with parental help
• Banking tools include ATM cards, netbanking, mobile apps, and UPI
• Apps like PhonePe, FamPay, and YONO help teens manage money digitally
• Always follow cyber safety rules to avoid fraud or data theft

Check Yourself – Mini Quiz

1. What is the main purpose of a savings account?
a) Taking loans
b) Paying EMI
c) Safely saving money and earning interest
d) Investing in stocks
Correct answer: c

2. Which of these tools helps you track your bank activity in paper format?
a) ATM Card
b) Passbook
c) Debit Card
d) Google Pay
Correct answer: b

3. True or False: You can open a bank account as a teen with a guardian's help.
Correct answer: True

Beyond the Book – Tools & Resources

Apps:
- YONO SBI
- HDFC Kids App
- PhonePe (UPI + wallet)
- FamPay (for 13–18-year-olds)

Websites to Explore:
- rbi.org.in – Learn banking basics
- npci.org.in – Know about UPI and digital banking
- bankofbaroda.in – Explore youth-friendly accounts

Watch:
• "How to Open a Bank Account for Students" – YouTube (India-specific guides)
• "UPI and Digital Payments Explained" – Simplified video by CA Rachana

Real Teen Voices

Kritika, 15 (Mumbai):
"I opened my account with my dad last year. Now, I save a part of every gift or allowance. It feels amazing to watch the balance grow!"
Rahil, 17 (Indore):
"Using UPI is convenient, but once I clicked on a fake cashback link and almost lost money. Always double-check before tapping."

Final Word

Banking is your first real step to financial independence.

It teaches you how to:
• Keep your money safe
• Access it smartly
• Track your savings
• Embrace digital tools
• Stay protected from fraud

You don't need to wait till college to learn how to use a bank. Start now. The earlier you begin, the more confident and empowered you'll feel when real financial responsibilities come your way.

Chapter 5

Saving for Goals

From Dream to Plan

Arjun dreams of buying a second-hand DSLR camera worth ₹20,000 to start a YouTube channel. He saves ₹500 a month from his tutoring income but doesn't know when he'll have enough. Sometimes he spends half of it on snacks or weekend outings with friends. He wonders, "Will I ever reach my goal?"

Sound familiar?

We all have dreams—big and small. But dreams stay dreams unless we turn them into goals and take steps to save consistently. This chapter shows you how to go from "I wish" to "I did it!"

Explore: Why Saving for Goals Matters

When you save for a specific purpose:

- You stay motivated to skip unnecessary expenses.
- You learn planning and patience.
- You build financial discipline that lasts a lifetime.

It's not just about buying things. It's about building habits that help you achieve life goals—college, travel, business, or helping your family.

What Is a Financial Goal?

A financial goal is something you want to achieve that requires money. It could be:

- **Short-term:** A new phone, game console, bike (0–6 months)
- **Medium-term:** Tuition for a coaching class, travel, laptop (6 months–2 years)
- **Long-term:** College education, study abroad, startup capital (2+ years)

From Dream to Plan – How to Set a Goal

Here's a 5-step plan you can use:

1. Define the Goal: What exactly do you want? Be clear.
Example: "Buy a DSLR camera for ₹20,000."
2. Decide the Deadline: By when do you want it?
"In 12 months."
3. Break It Down: Divide the amount by the months.
₹20,000 ÷ 12 = ₹1,667 per month
4. Track Your Progress: Use a journal or app to log each month.
5. Celebrate Milestones: Reward yourself for hitting monthly savings.

SMART Goals Framework

Make sure your goal is SMART:

Criteria	What It Means	Example
Specific	Clear and well-defined	"Save for DSLR camera"

Measurable	You can track progress	"₹20,000 in 12 months"
Achievable	Possible within your resources	"₹1,667/month from part-time job"
Realistic	Not too difficult or easy	"Cut snacks, save more"
Time-bound	Has a deadline	"By next June"

Goal-Saving Tools for Teens

Tool	**How It Helps**
Piggy Bank/Jar	For small savings at home
Bank Account	Keeps money safe, earns interest
Recurring Deposit (RD)	Monthly fixed savings, great for teens
Money Journal	Write down income, expenses, and savings
Apps like Walnut, Goodbudget	Visual budgeting and saving on your phone

Case Study: Priya's Laptop Plan

Goal: Buy a ₹40,000 laptop in 18 months for graphic design course.

Steps Taken:

- Started an RD account with ₹2,000/month.
- Skipped buying fast food; saved ₹500/month extra.
- Did freelance logo work for ₹1,000/month.
- Used a whiteboard to track savings visually.

Result: Priya hit ₹40,000 in 16 months and bought the laptop with pride.

Try It: Design Your Goal Tracker

Make your own savings chart:

• Draw a thermometer or ladder with ₹0 at the bottom and your target at the top.
• Each ₹500 or ₹1000 is one step.
• Colour in each step as you save.

OR use Google Sheets/Excel to make a table:

Month	Saved (₹)	Goal (₹)	Left to Save (₹)
July	1,500	20,000	18,500

Think & Reflect

• What is one thing I really want to buy or achieve in the next year?
• Can I set a timeline and create a savings plan?
• What can I cut down on to reach my savings goal faster?
• How would I feel if I achieved this on my own?

Let's Revise – Key Takeaways

• A goal gives your savings purpose and direction.
• Use the SMART goal method to stay focused.
• Break big dreams into small, monthly savings targets.
• Use tools like RDs, budget apps, goal charts to stay on track.
• Celebrate small wins and adjust your plan if needed.

Check Yourself – Quiz Time

1. What does the "T" in SMART goals stand for?

a) Tracking
b) Time-bound
c) Timeless

d) Targeted
Answer: b) Time-bound

2. Which of these is a long-term goal for a teen?
a) Buying a phone next week
b) Saving for college in 3 years
c) Going out with friends on Sunday
d) Getting a haircut
Answer: b) Saving for college in 3 years

3. True or False: Saving without a clear goal is just as effective as saving with one.
Answer: False

Beyond the Book – Tools & Resources

Apps for Tracking Goals:
• Goal Meter Habit Tracker (Android)
• Goodbudget – Simple envelope budgeting
• Money Lover – Teen-friendly budgeting app

Websites:
• www.groww.in – Explore simple investment plans
• rbi.org.in – Learn about savings and interest
• moneycontrol.com – Track financial goals and news

Videos to Watch:
• "How I Saved ₹1 Lakh by 18" – YouTube story
• "SMART Goals for Students" – Educational channels

Real Teen Voices

Vedant, 16 (Delhi):
"I always wanted a cycle but my parents said I'd have to save half the money. I started saving from tuition income, gave up ordering

online food, and reached my ₹5,000 target in six months."

Meher, 17 (Chennai):
"I created a money vision board for my dream of studying animation abroad. It keeps me focused and reminds me to save from my part-time content creation gig."

Final Word

Saving is not just about being careful—it's about being focused. When you set a goal, track it, and save regularly, you're telling the world, "I can achieve anything I work for."
So, whether it's a bike, laptop, college, or camera—start your plan today.
Because a goal without a plan is just a wish.

Chapter 6

Introduction to Investing

Grow Your Money Smarter

Meet Anaya, a 16-year-old student who recently received ₹10,000 as a birthday gift from her grandparents. Instead of spending it all, she wants to do something smart with the money. Her elder brother suggests she start investing. She's curious, "Isn't investing only for rich adults? What if I lose all my money?"

That's a common question.

But guess what? Investing is not just for grown-ups. In fact, the earlier you start, the greater your future returns can be. This chapter will help you understand what investing really means and how teens can start smart.

Explore: What is Investing?

Investing means using your money to buy something—like stocks, bonds, or mutual funds—with the goal that its value will grow over time.

It's different from saving. When you save, you store your money safely. When you invest, you put your money to work—so it can grow by itself.

Why Should You Start Investing Early?

- More time = more growth (thanks to compounding)
- Helps fight inflation (money losing value over time)
- Builds financial discipline
- Gives you a head-start on wealth creation

Think of investing like planting a tree. The sooner you plant it, the bigger it will grow.

The Power of Compounding

One of the most magical ideas in finance is compound interest. Let's say you invest ₹1,000 and it earns 10% a year. After one year, it becomes ₹1,100. In the second year, you earn interest not just on ₹1,000, but on ₹1,100.

Year	Amount (₹)
1	1,100
2	1,210
3	1,331
5	1,611
10	2,593

Now imagine investing ₹1,000 every year for 10 years. You'd have nearly ₹18,000 by the end, not ₹10,000.

Investing vs. Saving: What's the Difference?

Feature	Saving	Investing
Purpose	Safety, short-term goals	Growth, long-term goals
Return	Low (3–5%)	Higher (8–12% or more)
Risk Level	Very low	Medium to high
Time Horizon	Days to months	Years or decades
Examples	Savings account, FD	Mutual funds, stocks, gold

Try It: The 1 Lakh Challenge

Let's say you save ₹1,000 per month starting at age 15 and invest it with 10% return.

- **In 5 years:** You'll have ₹77,000+
- **In 10 years:** ₹2.1 lakhs+
- **In 20 years:** ₹6.8 lakhs+

If you wait until you're 25 to start, the difference is huge. That's the power of starting early.

Types of Basic Investment Options for Beginners

Here are the most beginner-friendly tools:

1. **Fixed Deposits (FD):**
    - o Safe
    - o Guaranteed returns (around 6–7%)
    - o Great for short-term saving

2. **Public Provident Fund (PPF):**
    - o Long-term
    - o Government-backed
    - o Lock-in of 15 years, but great interest (7–8%)

3. Mutual Funds via SIPs (Systematic Investment Plans):
- o You invest small amounts monthly
- o Professional fund managers handle the money
- o Medium to high return (8–12% average)

4. Gold:
- o Can be physical or digital
- o Good for long-term safety

5. Stocks:
- o You buy shares of companies like TCS, Infosys, Reliance
- o High risk, high return
- o Not advised without guidance for beginners

Where Can Teens Invest or Learn to Invest?

Since you may not be 18 yet, you'll need a guardian/parent to open an account in your name:

Option	What You Need
Mutual Funds	Guardian's PAN, Aadhaar
PPF Account	With parent in post office/bank
FD/RD	Minor account in bank
Stock Market	Demat account with guardian

Always ask a trusted adult and understand before investing.

Case Study: Rishabh's Mutual Fund Journey

Rishabh, 17, asked his parents to help him start a SIP of ₹1,000/ month in a balanced mutual fund. He continued for 2 years. At 19, when he needed money for his online course, the fund had grown to ₹28,000.
He didn't just save—it grew.

Think & Reflect

- If I had ₹1,000 today, would I spend or invest?
- What long-term goal could I work towards?
- Am I willing to be patient and let my money grow?
- Who can I talk to at home or school about investing safely?

Let's Revise – Key Takeaways

- Investing = growing your money over time with some level of risk.
- Start early to benefit from compounding.
- Understand the difference between saving (safe, low return) and investing (riskier, higher return).
- Mutual funds, PPFs, and FDs are good places to begin.
- Always learn before you invest and ask adults for help.

Check Yourself – Quiz

1. What is the biggest advantage of starting investing as a teenager?
a) You can skip budgeting
b) You avoid all risks
c) You have time on your side
d) You get free money
Answer: c) You have time on your side

2. Which of these has the highest risk but highest return?
a) Fixed Deposit
b) Savings Account
c) Mutual Fund
d) Stocks
Answer: d) Stocks

3. True or False: Compound interest means you earn interest on your interest.
Answer: True

Beyond the Book – Tools & Resources

Apps to Learn Investing:
- Fintoo
- Groww
- INDmoney

Websites:
- www.nseindia.com – Learn about stock market
- www.moneycontrol.com – Market trends and tips
- www.investopedia.com – Financial education

Videos to Watch:
- "Basics of Investing for Teenagers" – YouTube educational channels
- "SIP vs FD" – Learn the difference in returns

Real Teen Voices

Sanika, 16 (Nagpur):
"My dad helped me start a SIP. Now I'm saving for a graphic tablet to pursue design. Watching it grow every month is exciting!"

Aryan, 17 (Kolkata):
"Once I learned about compounding, I realized that even ₹500/month can grow big in 10 years. I'm in!"

Final Word

Investing isn't about luck. It's about planning, patience, and progress. Even a small step today becomes a big leap tomorrow.
The earlier you start investing, the faster your dreams can become reality.
So go ahead—talk to a trusted adult, pick your first investment, and watch your money grow smarter.

Chapter 7

Types of Investment Options

Pick What's Right for You

Imagine two friends, Zara and Ravi, both 17. Zara puts ₹1,000 in a fixed deposit and earns 6% interest. Ravi invests ₹1,000 in a mutual fund that earns 10%. After one year, Zara earns ₹60, while Ravi earns ₹100. Both invested the same amount—but their returns are different.

Why? Because different investments grow at different speeds—and carry different levels of risk and reward.

This chapter will help you understand and compare various investment options so you can decide what's best for your goals, comfort level, and future.

Explore: Investment Options 101

There are many ways to invest your money. Let's look at the most common types:

1. Fixed Deposit (FD)

Safety Level: Very Safe
Return: 5%–7%
Time Frame: 6 months to 10 years
A Fixed Deposit is when you lock your money in a bank for a fixed time and get a guaranteed interest.

• Great for short-term goals
• Ideal if you don't want to take any risks
• Available at all banks and post offices

Example: You invest ₹10,000 in an FD for 1 year at 6% → You get ₹10,600 at the end.

2. Recurring Deposit (RD)

Safety Level: Very Safe
Return: 5%–6.5%
Time Frame: 6 months to 10 years
You deposit a small amount every month, and the bank adds interest.

• Like a piggy bank with interest
• Great for students saving pocket money regularly

Example: ₹500/month for 1 year = ₹6,000 + interest = ~₹6,200

3. Public Provident Fund (PPF)

Safety Level: Extremely Safe (Govt. Backed)
Return: ~7% (compounded annually)
Time Frame: 15 years (long-term only)
Best for long-term saving with tax benefits. Money grows steadily.

• You can deposit from ₹500 to ₹1.5 lakh/year
• Early withdrawal allowed only under certain rules

Example: ₹1,000/month for 10 years can become ₹1.7–2 lakh+

4. Mutual Funds (via SIPs)

Safety Level: Low to High (depends on type)
Return: 8%–15% (not fixed)
Time Frame: Medium to long term (3–10+ years)
Mutual funds collect money from many investors and invest in shares, bonds, etc. SIP = investing monthly.

- Managed by professionals
- Best for teens starting small

Example: ₹1,000/month in SIP for 5 years → ~₹75,000–₹90,000

Types of Mutual Funds:

- Equity (high return, high risk)
- Debt (low risk, stable return)
- Balanced (mix of both)

5. Stock Market (Shares/Equity)

Safety Level: High Risk
Return: Can be high (>15%) but risky
Time Frame: Short to long term
Buying shares means owning a small part of a company. Prices go up or down every day.

- Requires knowledge and regular tracking
- Not ideal for beginners without guidance

Example: Buying 5 shares of a company at ₹200 → if it becomes ₹250, you earn ₹250
Note: Teens can invest through a guardian's Demat account.

6. Gold (Physical or Digital)

Safety Level: Safe
Return: 6%–10% (varies by market)

Time Frame: Medium to long term
Gold holds value and is used as a backup in emergencies.

- You can buy coins, jewellery, or digital gold
- Not affected by stock market directly

Example: Buying ₹5,000 worth of digital gold → Sell when price increases

7. Real Estate (Land, House)

Safety Level: Medium to high risk
Return: Long-term growth
Time Frame: 10+ years
Buying property is a big investment. Not suitable for teens, but good to know.

8. Crypto (Bitcoin, Ethereum, etc.)

Safety Level: Very High Risk
Return: Very high/very low (volatile)
Time Frame: Speculative
Cryptocurrencies are digital currencies. They're not regulated in India and can rise or fall quickly.

- Not recommended for teenagers
- Best to observe and learn, not invest

Tip: Learn about it through sandbox apps before jumping in.

Try It: Compare & Choose

Let's say you have ₹1,000/month to invest for 5 years. Based on average returns:

Investment	Estimated Value After 5 Years
Fixed Deposit (6%)	₹6,800–₹7,000
PPF (7.1%)	₹7,100–₹7,400

Mutual Fund SIP (10%)	₹7,800–₹8,200
Gold (avg. 8%)	₹7,400–₹7,800

Which one would you choose and why?

Think & Reflect

- Do I want safe returns or higher returns with risk?
- Am I saving for 1 year, 5 years, or longer?
- Do I need quick access to my money?
- What kind of investment matches my personality?

Let's Revise – Key Takeaways

- There are many investment options—each with different risk, return, and time horizons.
- Safe options = FD, RD, PPF
- Growth options = Mutual Funds, Stocks
- Start small, choose wisely, and always learn before investing
- Choose what aligns with your goals and comfort level

Check Yourself – Quiz

1. Which investment has the longest lock-in period?
a) Fixed Deposit
b) Mutual Fund
c) PPF
d) Gold
Answer: c) PPF

2. What does SIP stand for?
a) Savings Insurance Plan
b) Systematic Investment Plan
c) Safe Income Portfolio
Answer: b) Systematic Investment Plan

3. True or False: All mutual funds give guaranteed returns.
Answer: False

Beyond the Book – Tools & Resources

Websites:

- www.moneycontrol.com – Compare returns
- www.nsc.gov.in – PPF & RD rules
- www.groww.in – Mutual fund info

Apps:

- Kuvera
- Groww
- Coin by Zerodha

YouTube Channels:

- CA Rachana Ranade
- Pranjal Kamra
- Labour Law Advisor (Hindi)

Real Teen Voice

Mehul, 16 (Pune):
"I started a SIP with my parents' help. It's exciting to watch it grow every month. I even track it using an app."

Final Word

There's no one-size-fits-all in investing. Some prefer safety. Others want growth. The trick is to match your investment to your goal, time, and comfort with risk. Even if you don't start today, learning about these options gives you power. When the time comes, you'll be ready to grow your money wisely.

Chapter 8

Financial Planning for Education and Career

Secure Your Dreams with Smart Planning

Meet Ananya, a 16-year-old who dreams of studying computer science at a top university. She Googles the course fees—₹10 to ₹20 lakhs! Her excitement fades. "Where will I get this much money?" But then, her elder cousin advises her, "Start planning now—save smartly, apply for scholarships, and explore education loans."
This chapter shows how planning for education and career is not just for adults—it's something every teen can and should do early.

Explore: Why You Need to Plan Ahead

Whether you dream of becoming a doctor, artist, pilot, or entrepreneur—your career goals require planning, and that includes money.

Why Financial Planning for Education Matters:

• Helps you estimate costs of your education journey

• Reduces the burden on parents or guardians
• Encourages you to look for smart options—like scholarships or low-cost alternatives
• Keeps you motivated with a clear vision

Career Goals Have Price Tags:
• College tuition
• Coaching or entrance exam fees
• Study materials or laptop
• Hostel/transportation
• Living expenses

When you plan ahead, you're in control.

Try It: Estimate Your Future Education Cost

Here's an example for a student wanting to pursue Engineering (B.Tech) at a reputed college:

Item	Estimated Cost (4 years)
Tuition Fees	₹6,00,000 – ₹10,00,000
Hostel & Mess	₹2,00,000 – ₹3,00,000
Books, Laptop, Supplies	₹1,00,000 – ₹1,50,000
Coaching (JEE prep, etc.)	₹1,00,000 – ₹2,00,000
Miscellaneous	₹50,000
Total	₹10,50,000 – ₹16,00,000

Now YOU try:
Think of the career you want. Use college websites or talk to seniors and fill out your version of this table. It's your first step to smart financial planning!

Explore: Sources of Funding

Once you know your target, look at the sources to reach it.

1. Personal/Family Savings

- Open a savings account dedicated to college fund
- Set monthly goals (e.g., ₹500–₹1000)
- Ask relatives to contribute on birthdays instead of gifts!

2. Scholarships & Grants

- Central and state government scholarships (e.g., NSP portal)
- Private and corporate scholarships (e.g., Tata Trusts, Reliance Foundation)
- College-specific merit-based scholarships
- Check eligibility: academic marks, family income, special categories

Tip: Keep a list of scholarship deadlines. Start applying in Class 10 or 11 itself.

3. Part-Time Jobs or Internships

- Freelancing, tutoring, blogging, coding gigs
- Save a portion for your college fund

4. Education Loans

- Available from banks (e.g., SBI, HDFC, BoB)
- Repayment begins after the course ends
- Interest subsidy available for low-income families (via CSIS)

5. Crowdfunding

- Some students use trusted platforms (like Ketto or Milaap) to raise funds—especially for higher education abroad.

Goal-Setting Template

Let's break your career dream into a SMART financial goal:

SMART Goal Element	Example: Becoming a Graphic Designer
Specific	Save ₹2 lakhs for diploma fees
Measurable	Save ₹2,000/month for 24 months
Achievable	Earn through designing posters online
Realistic	Affordable course + part-time work
Time-Bound	Reach goal by June 2027

Your Turn: Fill this out for your own dream path!

Think & Reflect

- Have you talked to your parents about college expenses?
- Are you relying only on them, or are you trying to contribute too?
- What would motivate you to save now for your future?
- Which scholarships or entrance exams are you preparing for?

Let's Revise – Key Points

- Financial planning is essential for your career goals
- Break large goals into actionable savings and funding steps
- Use scholarships, part-time income, and loans wisely
- Apply the SMART goal framework to stay on track

Check Yourself – Quiz

1. Which of the following is a loan you pay back after education?

a) Grant

b) Education Loan

c) Scholarship
Answer: b) Education Loan

2. What is one benefit of a SMART goal?
a) It guarantees success
b) It helps create a clear, focused plan
Answer: b) It helps create a clear, focused plan

3. True or False: You should only start planning your education finances after Class 12.
Answer: False

Beyond the Book – Tools & Resources

Websites:
- https://scholarships.gov.in – National Scholarship Portal
- https://vidyalakshmi.co.in – Apply for education loans
- CollegeDunia.com, Shiksha.com – Compare college costs

Apps:
- Buddy4Study (scholarship alerts)
- Groww (goal-based investing)

TED Talks:
- "Why You Will Fail to Have a Great Career" – Larry Smith
- "What Adults Can Learn From Kids" – Adora Svitak

Real Teen Voice

Ishaan, 17 (Delhi):
"I want to become a software engineer. I saved up for a coding course by making Instagram reels for local businesses. That was my first career investment!"

Activity: Build Your Career-Finance Tracker

Make a 3-column table:

Career Goal	Cost Estimate	Saving/Funding Plan

Update it every 3 months to see progress. Add notes like deadlines, scholarships applied, or exam dates.

Final Thoughts

Your future is a combination of dreams + action + planning. And part of that action is financial planning—not just relying on parents, but being financially aware, responsible, and involved.
Even saving ₹100 a week or researching scholarships is a step forward.

Remember: You don't have to be rich to chase big goals—you just have to be smart and strategic.

Chapter 9

Avoiding Debt and Bad Habits

Stay Ahead by Staying Smart

Meet Neha, a 17-year-old who just got her first prepaid card. Excited, she starts spending on trendy clothes, online food, and gaming apps. At the end of the month, she's shocked to find her balance empty—and worse, she owes her cousin ₹2000 for a borrowed splurge.
Sound familiar?
Welcome to the world of spending traps. Teenagers like Neha often fall into debt or bad financial habits not because they're careless, but because no one taught them how to manage money the smart way. This chapter is your safety shield.

Explore: What Is Debt and Why It Can Be Dangerous

Debt means borrowing money that you promise to repay, usually with interest. While some types of debt (like education loans or home loans) can be helpful, bad debt—like credit card dues or personal loans for luxuries—can pull you into a financial mess.

Types of Debt You Should Know:

Type of Debt	What It Is	Risk Level
Credit Card Debt	Borrowed money with high interest	High
Personal Loan	Unsecured loan from bank or app	High
Education Loan	Loan for college/study, paid after course	Medium
EMI Buy Now, Pay Later	Split payment services (e.g., ZestMoney)	Medium
Payday Loans/Apps	Instant cash apps—often risky and unregulated	Very High

The Real Cost of Debt

Let's say you borrow ₹5,000 on a credit card with 36% annual interest.

If you don't repay in 1 year:
You'll owe over ₹1,800 in interest! That's almost 40% extra.
Debt grows fast. If you only pay the minimum amount, you'll stay trapped much longer.

Common Bad Financial Habits (And How to Break Them)

1. Impulse Buying

o Buying something you don't need just because it's trending or on sale.

o **Fix:** Use the 24-hour rule. Wait one day before any non-essential purchase.

2. Peer Pressure Spending

o "Everyone has the new iPhone, I want one too!"
o **Fix:** Track your goals. Be proud of being different—and responsible.

3. Spending More Than You Earn

o Using credit or borrowing when allowance/income is not enough.
o **Fix:** Stick to a budget. Save first, spend later.

4. Ignoring Small Debts

o Thinking "It's just ₹500"—until it adds up to ₹5000.
o **Fix:** Pay off small debts quickly. Avoid accumulating dues.

Try It: Good Debt vs. Bad Debt Scenario

Scenario A: You borrow ₹10,000 for a certified online course in graphic design that helps you freelance.

Scenario B: You borrow ₹10,000 to buy expensive shoes to impress your friends.

Which one is a good debt? Why?
Discuss in class or write in your money journal.

Digital Debt Dangers for Teens

• Many teens use BNPL (Buy Now Pay Later) apps like LazyPay, Simpl, etc.
• They seem easy—but every missed payment affects your credit score.
• Some apps use aggressive recovery tactics or hidden charges.
• Always read the terms before clicking "Pay Later".

Tip: Never borrow from apps or sites that are not RBI-registered.

Think & Reflect

- Have you ever borrowed money from someone? Why?
- What did it feel like to owe money?
- Are there times you regretted a purchase?
- How can you avoid financial stress in your college or work life?

Golden Rule: Live Below Your Means

This doesn't mean you should never enjoy life.
It means: spend less than you earn and save the rest for your dreams.

Use the 50-30-20 Rule:
- 50% for needs (school, food, transport)
- 30% for wants (fun, entertainment)
- 20% for savings/investments

Let's Revise – Key Takeaways

- Debt is borrowing money that you must repay, often with interest.
- Avoid bad habits like impulse spending, peer pressure buying, or ignoring debts.
- Not all debt is bad—but it must be planned and manageable.
- Always read the fine print of any loan, BNPL or credit product.
- Use the 50-30-20 rule to manage your income wisely.

Check Yourself – Quiz

1. What is the major risk of using credit cards without paying the full amount each month?
a) Cashback offers
b) Higher credit score
c) High interest charges
Answer: c) High interest charges

2. Which of the following is a good financial habit?
a) Spending more than you earn
b) Budgeting monthly expenses
c) Taking loans for luxury shopping
Answer: b) Budgeting monthly expenses

3. True or False: Buy Now Pay Later options are always safe for teenagers.
Answer: False

Beyond the Book – Tools & Resources

Apps to Track Spending & Avoid Overspending:
• Walnut
• Money Manager
• Google Sheets Budget Template

Helpful Videos:
• "How to Avoid Debt" – YouTube (Money School)
• "Minimalism and Money" – TEDx Talk

Books:
• I Will Teach You to Be Rich (Teen Edition) by Ramit Sethi
• The Psychology of Money by Morgan Housel (simple chapters)

Real Teen Story

Shreya, 16 (Lucknow):
"I once used a BNPL app for clothes and forgot to repay. The calls and late fees scared me. That experience made me set a strict monthly budget. Now I track everything on an app—and never borrow for shopping!"

Activity: Break Your Bad Habits

Fill this table in your notebook:

Habit to Break	Why it's harmful	Replacement Good Habit

Example:
| Impulse Shopping | Wastes money & regret | Wait 24 hours before buying |

Final Thoughts

Bad financial habits and unplanned debt don't just hurt your wallet—they impact your peace of mind and your future dreams.
As a teen, you have the perfect time to set great habits.
Learn to say "no" to what doesn't serve your future.

Smart teens don't just earn money—they protect it.

Chapter 10

Smart Money Habits for Life

Build a Financial Future You'll Be Proud Of

Arjun, a 17-year-old from Pune, recently started earning through freelance video editing. Excited by his new income, he began splurging on gadgets, games, and snacks. One month later—he had nothing left. No savings, no plan, no idea where his money went. Now imagine if Arjun had a few smart money habits from the start. What if he knew how to save, spend wisely, and plan for the unexpected?

In this chapter, we'll explore how to build lifelong financial habits that create peace of mind, confidence, and independence.

Explore: What Are Smart Money Habits?

Money habits are the routines and choices you make with your finances—how you earn, spend, save, invest, and give. Good habits grow wealth. Bad habits drain it.

Smart money habits help you:

- Avoid debt
- Grow your savings
- Invest in your dreams
- Stay calm in emergencies
- Build long-term financial success

The 7 Smartest Money Habits to Start Now

1. Pay Yourself First

Before spending anything, save a portion of your income.

Tip: Start with 20% savings every time you receive money. Automate it if possible.

2. Track Every Rupee

Keep a record of your expenses—daily or weekly.
Use apps like Walnut, Goodbudget, or a simple Google Sheet.

3. Create a Monthly Budget

Know your income and break it into needs, wants, and savings.

Follow the 50-30-20 rule:

- 50% Needs
- 30% Wants
- 20% Savings

4. Set SMART Goals

Whether it's saving for a phone or college, goals should be:
Specific, Measurable, Achievable, Realistic, and Time-bound.

5. Build an Emergency Fund

Save money for unexpected events—illness, tech failure, or a last-minute trip.
Start with ₹1,000–₹5,000 in a separate account.

6. Learn Before You Spend

Before buying or investing, do your research.

Ask: Is this a need or a want? Will I use it for more than 3 months?

7. Give Back

Help your community with donations or time. It builds empathy and financial mindfulness.

Bonus Habits

• Stay Away from Peer Pressure Purchases

Just because friends are buying something doesn't mean you need it too.

• Think Long-Term

Ask: Will this help me 6 months or 1 year from now?

• Protect Your Data and Money Online

Use strong passwords. Don't share OTPs. Use only verified apps.

Try It: Build Your Personal Habit Tracker

Date	**Saved ₹**	**Tracked Expenses?**	**No Impulse Buys?**	Notes
July 1	₹200	✔	✔	Great start!

Try this for one week. See what changes.

Think & Reflect

• What's your weakest money habit right now?

• What one small change can you make today?

• Who do you know that has great money habits? What can you learn from them?

Mistakes to Avoid

Mistake	Smart Habit Replacement
Spending without tracking	Use a daily expense log
Living paycheck to paycheck	Automate savings first
Relying on others for emergencies	Build your emergency fund
Buying to impress friends	Set personal financial goals

Tools to Build Habits

Apps:

- Money Lover – Budget planner and expense tracker
- Goal Tracker – Set savings targets
- PocketGuard – Monitors spending and savings

Planners & Journals:

- Bullet journals for goals
- Printable savings trackers
- Budget envelopes for cash use

Real Teen Story

Aaliya, 18 (Delhi):

"I used to spend all my allowance in the first week. Then I started a journal and wrote every rupee I spent. I was shocked! Now, I use the 50-30-20 rule and save for short trips with my friends. I feel proud and independent."

Let's Revise – Key Points

- Smart money habits build a smart financial future
- Pay yourself first and always track your expenses
- Use the 50-30-20 rule for budgeting

• Emergency funds are a must—even for teens
• Avoid peer pressure and think long-term
• Use apps, planners, or journals to stay on track

Check Yourself – Quiz

1. What does "Pay Yourself First" mean?
a) Spend on needs before savings
b) Save money before spending
c) Pay your parents
Answer: b) Save money before spending

2. What is the 50-30-20 budgeting rule used for?
a) Planning meals
b) Budgeting income into needs, wants, savings
c) Investing in stocks
Answer: b)

3. True or False: Emergency funds are only for adults.
Answer: False

4. What's a SMART goal?
A goal that is Specific, Measurable, Achievable, Realistic, Time-bound

Beyond the Book – Learn More

Websites:
• www.investopedia.com – Beginner money terms
• RBI's Money Smart – Indian banking concepts

TED Talks:
• "Why You Should Start Saving Young"
• "The Secret to Lifelong Financial Wellness"

YouTube Channels:

- CA Rachana Ranade
- Labour Law Advisor – Youth finance

Books:

- The Barefoot Investor for Teens
- Rich Dad Poor Dad – Teen Edition

Final Thought

Money isn't just about numbers—it's about freedom, confidence, and choices.

If you build strong money habits now, they'll carry you through every phase of life. Whether you become a doctor, entrepreneur, artist, or teacher—your financial future is in your hands.

Start small. Stay consistent. Think long-term.

Chapter 11

Digital Payments and Online Safety

Your Guide to Safe, Smart Online Money Moves

Tanya, a 16-year-old student from Lucknow, just bought a concert ticket online using her mom's UPI ID. Minutes later, she received a call saying her transaction failed and she had to "verify her OTP." She gave the code—₹5,000 was gone from her mom's bank account. She'd been scammed. This is not rare.

As teenagers embrace digital wallets, UPI, and mobile banking, knowing how to use them wisely and safely is essential. In this chapter, we'll help you become a smart and secure digital money user.

Explore: What Are Digital Payments?

Digital payment is the process of paying or receiving money electronically—no cash or cheques involved.

Common digital payment methods in India:

Method	Description
UPI	Unified Payments Interface – instant transfers via apps like Google Pay, PhonePe, Paytm
Debit/Credit Cards	Bank cards for online or POS purchases
Mobile Wallets	Apps that store money – Paytm, Amazon Pay, etc.
Net Banking	Banking through websites or apps
QR Codes	Scan-and-pay method popular in shops

India leads globally in real-time digital payments (thanks to UPI).

Why Are Digital Payments Important for Teens?

- Convenience – Pay, recharge, or shop from your phone
- Trackability – Automatic records of transactions
- Financial independence – Learn to manage small purchases
- Future readiness – Digital is the norm in careers, education, and travel

The Flip Side – Risks You Must Know

Risk	Example
Scams & Fraud	Fake calls, links, or apps stealing money
Data Theft	Personal info hacked from insecure apps
Over-spending	Easy tap-to-pay leads to impulse buys
Privacy Issues	Apps collecting more data than needed

Smart Digital Payment Tips for Teens

Use Trusted Apps Only

Stick to verified UPI apps like:

- Google Pay

• PhonePe
• Paytm
• BHIM

Avoid installing random payment apps from social media or SMS.

Set App Locks & Passwords
• Use App Lock on financial apps
• Set strong passwords (not your name/birthday)
• Enable 2-Factor Authentication (2FA)

Never Share OTP or UPI PIN
• Even with friends or strangers claiming to be "bank officials"
• No real bank ever asks for your OTP or PIN

Scan QR Codes Carefully
• Only scan QR codes from trusted stores or websites
• Check spelling of UPI IDs—fraudsters often use small changes (like @paytmm vs @paytm)

Track All Transactions
Check your transaction history regularly. If something looks wrong, report it immediately.

Cyber Hygiene Checklist

Habit	Do You Follow It?
Only use apps from Google Play/App Store	✗ / ✔
Lock your phone with a PIN or fingerprint	✗ / ✔
Regularly update apps	✗ / ✔
Avoid public Wi-Fi for banking	✗ / ✔
Never click on suspicious links	✗ / ✔

How many ✔ do you have?

Try It: Spot the Scam Activity

Which of these is a scam?
A) A message says you won ₹10,000 and asks to click a link.

B) Your UPI app asks for your PIN before sending money.

C) You receive a call from someone claiming to be from RBI asking for your Aadhaar number.

Answers: A & C are scams. RBI never calls individuals.

Real Teen Story

Rohan, 17 (Mumbai):
"I once tried to buy headphones via an Instagram ad. I paid via UPI, but the seller disappeared. Now, I only buy from trusted websites and avoid random payment links."

Think & Reflect

- Have you ever clicked a suspicious link or shared an OTP?
- What do you do if your friend asks to use your UPI ID?
- Are you prepared to handle online money safely?

Let's Revise – Key Points

- Digital payments include UPI, wallets, debit cards, and more
- India is a leader in real-time digital transactions
- With convenience comes the risk of fraud and scams
- Teens should use only trusted apps and follow safety tips
- Never share your OTP, PIN, or bank info
- Practicing cyber hygiene is crucial for financial safety

Check Yourself – Quiz

1. What does UPI stand for?
a) Unified Payment Interface
b) Unlimited Payment Internet
c) Unique Private Identity
Answer: a)

2. What should you do if someone asks for your OTP?
a) Give it if they say they're from the bank
b) Say no and report the number
c) Share it with your friend
Answer: b)

3. True or False: Using public Wi-Fi for banking is safe.
Answer: False

4. Which is NOT a digital payment method?
a) Credit Card
b) QR Code
c) Cheque
Answer: c)

Beyond the Book – Resources

Websites & Apps
• www.cybercrime.gov.in – Report digital fraud
• RBI's Digital Literacy Site
• Truecaller App – Identify spam callers

YouTube
• Cyber Safety Tips for Teens – National Cyber Security
• RBI's UPI Security Explained

Books

- Internet Safety for Kids & Teens
- The Teen's Guide to Digital Life

TED Talks

- How to Outsmart a Hacker – Keren Elazari
- The Future of Digital Payments – Nandan Nilekani

Final Word

The internet has made money management easier—but also riskier. As a teenager, you're a prime target for fraud—but you also have the power to protect yourself.

Being smart with digital payments is not about fear—it's about freedom and confidence.
Stay alert. Stay safe. Stay smart.

Chapter 12

Creating Passive Income and Entrepreneurship Basics

Earn While You Sleep – The Teen Guide to Making Money Smarter

Ishaan loves gaming. He streams videos on YouTube and makes ₹1,000 a month from ads. His friend Meher sells handmade jewelry on Instagram. Both are in high school—and both are earning while learning. Welcome to the world of passive income and teenpreneurship—where your ideas, hobbies, and creativity can become money-makers.

You don't need a degree or office. You need a mindset, skills, and a little bit of hustle.

Explore: What Is Passive Income?

Passive income is money you earn without working all the time for it. It's different from a part-time job, where you earn only when you work.

Think of it like a tree: you plant the seed (effort), water it (time), and later it gives you fruit (income) even if you're not working on it every day.

Common Passive Income Sources for Teens:

Source	Description
YouTube Channel	Create videos, earn from ads
Blogging or Writing	Monetize through ads or affiliate links
Print-on-Demand	Design T-shirts, mugs online and earn per sale
E-books	Write and sell stories, notes, or guides
Stock Photography	Upload photos and earn royalty
Digital Products	Sell templates, planners, art, music
Tutoring Apps	Record lessons and earn per view

What Is Teen Entrepreneurship?

Entrepreneurship means starting a small business or service using your skills, passion, or solution to a problem. Teen entrepreneurs (or teenpreneurs!) build real businesses—online or offline—while still in school.

Why Start Young?

- You have more time to experiment
- You learn real-world money & life skills
- Failures are lessons, not disasters
- You build confidence, independence, and a portfolio

Startup Ideas for Students

Category	Ideas
Skill-Based	Graphic design, coding, tutoring, photography

Product-Based	Handmade crafts, home-baked goods, art prints
Service-Based	Pet walking, resume writing, podcast editing
Digital	Create apps, design websites, manage social media
Educational	Sell your class notes or test prep guides

Choose something you're passionate about + has a market need.

Try It: Start Your First Micro-Startup

Step 1: Brainstorm Your Idea
• What are your skills or interests?
• What do people often ask you for help with?

Step 2: Validate It
• Ask friends, family, or classmates: "Would you pay for this?"

Step 3: Name It & Set a Goal
• Fun name, logo, simple business plan
• Decide how much time and money you'll invest

Step 4: Go Live
• Set up Instagram, Google Form, or WhatsApp
• Start small, get feedback, improve

Step 5: Track & Learn
• Maintain a sales tracker or journal
• Celebrate your wins, learn from your flops

Think & Reflect

• What's one hobby of yours that could earn money?
• How would you balance school and a side hustle?

• What scares you about starting something on your own?
"You don't have to be great to start. But you have to start to be great." – Zig Ziglar

Protecting Your Ideas & Work

As you go digital, always:
• Copyright your original designs
• Add watermarks to photos/art
• Never share full personal info online
• Use payment gateways (like Razorpay or Instamojo) instead of personal bank details

Let's Revise – Key Points

• Passive income = money you earn even while sleeping
• Teens can start with content, services, or digital products
• Entrepreneurship is about solving problems creatively
• Start small, fail fast, learn big
• Protect your digital identity and intellectual property

Check Yourself – Quiz

1. What is passive income?
a) Income from working full-time
b) Money earned with little ongoing effort
c) Money from school scholarships
Answer: b)

2. Which is NOT a passive income source?
a) Salary from a job
b) Selling your e-book online
c) YouTube ad earnings
Answer: a)

3. True or False: You must be 18+ to start a business.
Answer: False

4. Which platform is best for selling handmade crafts?
a) LinkedIn
b) Instagram or Etsy
c) Google Docs
Answer: b)

Beyond the Book – Resources

Websites
- Teen Business Guide – www.bizkids.com
- Razorpay – Payment Gateway for Small Businesses
- Meesho – Resell Products from Home

Apps
- Canva (for logo/poster making)
- InShot (video editing)
- Shopify (start your store)
- Trello or Notion (business planning)

Inspiration
- Kidpreneurs by Adam Toren (book)
- YouTube: Teen Entrepreneurs of India series
- Instagram: Follow @Funngro (teen earning platform)

TED Talks
- What Adults Can Learn from Kids – Adora Svitak
- Starting a Business at Age 14 – Maya Penn

Final Word

You're not "too young" to earn or create. Whether it's designing bookmarks or editing reels, your skill + action = power.

Your first rupee from your idea is the beginning of a life-changing journey.

So go ahead—dream it, test it, build it.

Your pocket money isn't the only money you can make.

Summary

"Smart Teen Ki Smart Money Guide" is a complete resource to help teenagers (Grades 9–12) become financially confident. Through real-life stories, activities, and practical examples, readers learn how to earn, save, budget, and invest money wisely.

The book begins with the basics of money management and gradually introduces more complex concepts like investing, loans, credit cards, digital safety, and entrepreneurship. Each chapter ends with reflection prompts, quizzes, and real-world tools.

By the end, students are equipped to:

- Create a personal budget
- Set financial goals
- Save for education and future needs
- Avoid common money traps
- Launch a small business or passive income idea
- Plan for a financially smart future

Glossary (Selected Terms)

- Budget – A plan for how to earn and spend money.

- Compound Interest – Earning interest on both the original amount and the interest already earned.

- Credit Score – A number that shows how well you handle borrowing and repaying money.

- Debt – Money that you owe to someone else.

- Emergency Fund – Savings set aside for unexpected expenses.

- Investment – Putting money into something (like stocks or mutual funds) to grow it over time.

- Passive Income – Income earned with little ongoing effort, like YouTube revenue or selling digital products.

- SIP (Systematic Investment Plan) – A way to invest small amounts regularly in mutual funds.

- UPI (Unified Payments Interface) – A digital system in India that lets you send and receive money instantly using mobile apps.